“Being single doesn’t mean you’re weak, it means you’re strong enough to wait for what you deserve…’

Cover design by Samantha Thorne Design.

Internet dating, it's not for everyone.
It's tough, but it certainly has its interesting moments.
It's a bit like spaghetti, you keep throwing it at the wall until something sticks.

I've spent the last year keeping a diary about my most amusing dates, good and bad. My work friends used to eagerly await my next date, so they could hear the stories I had to tell, and they were the ones who told me that I should write a book because you just couldn't make this stuff up. So, I did.

It's just a small insight into the world of modern day online dating and the type of people you could potentially meet. Sometimes I felt like the only normal person out there. Maybe whilst reading this you'll find that you have also had similar dating experiences.

I've learnt new phrases like catfishing and ghosting and experienced some of them first-hand. or you may be thinking about dabbling in the world of internet dating and want to know some of the things that you may encounter if you decide to do so. Either way, I guess this is just a tongue in cheek snippet of my life for the last year. I have enjoyed it at times, but it has also been as equally frustrating, but I guess it is true to say that internet dating has never been boring.

And you're not allowed to skip to the end to find out if I'm sitting like Bridget Jones crying into my cereal, or if I'm deliriously happy and have met the man of my dreams...

MY JOURNEY...

"Hi, I'm from Sidcup, 6ft4 and big down below, fancy a chat"

My internet dating journey began in April 2017, not long after I had spilt from my 2nd husband (who I coincidentally met on an online dating site 6 years previously but that's a whole different story, and one that isn't nearly as amusing as the encounters in this book).

Finding myself single and rapidly approaching 40, it seemed like now would be a good time to step into the world of internet dating once again. So, with much trepidation, a little hope, and a very thick skin, I took the plunge.

A lot of my single friends have tried internet dating in the past, and they have run screaming for the hills within minutes; it's not for the faint of heart that's for sure.

"Im an ex porn star, I'm well endowed you should know, fancy a chat?"

I've discovered most of the men on these sites can be placed into the following categories: players, time wasters, dick heads, married men, perverts, weirdo's, fakes and trolls. I apologise, at this stage, to the other 5%, the normal and nice genuine guys who I did have the pleasure to meet and talk to.

There are a few, don't get me wrong, I have met some lovely, sweet guys but when that spark just isn't there, then you may as well be dating a wet fish. So, unfortunately those genuine and nice guys probably won't make it into this book.

"Hi, my name's Scott, I'm here with my friend Clare and we'd really like to chat and go on a date sometime"

It is all the other creeps that I have met or spoke with that have inspired me to keep a diary of the horror stories I was encountering on a regular basis.

I see it as karma, if you are a nice and respectable man and you treated me with respect, the I was nice enough to not include you in this book. Alternatively, if you were a dick, well you lucky thing… you're in! You're welcome.

"Big boobs. Wow. Whoops"

"You're a fake no doubt"

DATING LIKE A MAN....

When I first begun online dating again, I did so with such optimism and full of hope that there would be a big wide world full of Prince Charming's, all there and ready to sweep in and make all of my dating dreams come true. After six months that perception is in tatters, I'm sorry to say.

When I first joined the world of online dating, again, it was whilst I was on holiday, sitting by the pool. I made my profile and the messages started pouring in. When you're new on there the men jump on you like a dog in heat. You're like the new kid on the block and everyone wants to know you. Although I personally didn't want to be having multiple conversations, and within hours of joining I began chatting to a guy and I continued to chat to just that one person for the whole of my holiday, effectively ignoring the rest of my inbox. We met up on my return, and after one date it turned out that it just wasn't meant to be. And gradually over the last six months I'm afraid to say that I have stopped dating like that and instead I've started dating like a man.

"So your tallist then, so shallow"

I keep my options open, I talk to various people, and I have message flying back and forth, and I try to juggle it all. Why? Because I've been let down more times than I can remember. Tonight, whilst I am writing this, it just so happens that it is one of those nights; it is 6pm on a Saturday evening, I've showered and got myself half ready to meet up with a new date, and then I get a text saying he's got a hangover and he can't make it. Whether that was true or not, I'll never know but it's certainly not the first time that I have been blown off at the last minute. I'm guessing that it's because men are so greedy and they think the grass is greener, they probably got themselves a better offer.

I have often compared it to girl's when they are dress shopping: you go in the first shop and you find and try on an amazing dress, but a part of you thinks no, there may be a better one. So, you trawl every shop trying on loads of ill-fitting dresses, and then you finally realise that the first dress was actually absolutely perfect. So, you go back to that first shop only to find that your dream dress has already been bought by someone else! I like to think that I am that dress, it makes me feel better anyway, when I think that all the guys that screwed up then tried to come crawling back. It gives my ego a little boost when I think that I am that amazing dress that so many lost out on.

And now, I guess I do the same as the men do, and rather than putting all of my eggs in one basket,

"I'm only 5ft10 but I own a Bentley"

I'm guessing the car makes up for your small penis too?

I instead spread them around a bit in the hope that one of those guys will actually turn out to be a genuine one. I'm not proud of this style of dating, and it's certainly not who I am as a person; I'm very loyal and certainly not a player, but I think this is the effect that online dating has had on me. I have found that it makes you so much more cautious and more wary of people's intentions.

"If I wear heels I'd be the man of your dreams"

If I punch you in the face will you go away

So, do I get disappointed when I get let down, of course I do. Do I also bounce back pretty quickly these days, hell yeah! You almost expect it, so that when it does happen it's like a little voice in your head says: see, I told you that was going to happen!

I will admit that I have dated a lot, not only during this current year, but 6 years ago as well, before I met my ex. I have lots of stories to tell. My work colleagues seem to really enjoy hearing my dating tales, and although I'm sure they would be pleased for me if I were to meet someone and settle down, I do also think they would be slightly disappointed that they'd no longer have me amusing them with my dates from hell stories.

"Can we go out for a drink? I have something to show you..."

Well, that's not creepy...

I do come and go from the site though because it can become tedious. Sometimes you need a break so that you can gather yourself together so that you're ready to battle it all again. I do get lots of messages, and more often than not they are deleted. Then I get abuse for that too. If you reply and say thanks but you're not right for me, good luck in your search, it then opens you up to a conversation about what's wrong with them. If you ignore them you then also get abuse for that, and apparently that also means that you're up your own arse.

"Wow, you're tall."

Really?! I haven't spent most of my adult life noticing that! Weird!

When it comes to my dating choices, the main criteria for me, being 6ft tall myself, is to meet a tall guy; a very large high heeled shoe collection is too important to sacrifice, even for someone like Brad Pitt. So, 6ft3 and above is something that I make VERY clear in my profile. Although I quickly discovered that most men don't know how to read and just look at your pictures instead.
As a result, my delete button gets used rather frequently on short arsed men that say, 'nice profile', when what they really mean is 'I gawped at your photos.'
And if I had a pound for every time someone suggested Cuban heels or said that we are all the same laying down, then I wouldn't be writing this, I would be off in some luxurious location with a hot man on my arm, of course! Sorry, I'm

"I'm not tall, does it matter?"

Nah, course not, I can just rest my arm on your head when were out, yeah?

getting distracted by dream world, it's a place that I frequently like to visit. It's an amazing place where, some tall and hunky Romeo has swept me off my feet and is treating me like a princess. There's plenty of cocktails and sunshine, and there's enough shoes to last a lifetime as well, and of course there will be an endless supply of chocolate, flowers and romance.

But back to reality, I'm sitting in my lounge with a cup of tea seeing what my dating inbox has in store for me today. I've already had some keyboard warrior summarise that I am a player without even speaking to me. That's another one blocked! A few more saying, 'wow, you're tall'. Or you're shallow (he's 5ft2 by the way, with short man syndrome). Oh, lovely, and one asking what size my boobs are. There are some classy men on here today. I'm going back to my dream world...

MY DREAM MAN

(WE'RE STAYING IN DREAM WORLD FOR A WHILE)

"How would you feel about me throttling you during sex to the point you pass out then I fuck you"

Erm, I think that's called sexual assault!

Well, he would be very tall, at least 6ft3, and I also like a guy that takes care of himself but who isn't too obsessed either. I like the gym, but there is nothing worse than an unhealthy obsession with it. I love tattoos on a man; they are my weakness. I also like a good head of hair that is preferably in a trendy style. Nice teeth are also always a good bonus, and it's always a win if they smell nice. My best friend, Lauren, often smells men, and not subtly either. It's kind of her thing, smelling people – such a weirdo! I do also like a man that dresses well, but that is something that can be worked on. As long as they don't dress like my dad then there is hope.

> *"Do you believe in one-night stands?"*
>
> *Do you believe in miracles?*

I do think that I'd like to meet someone who doesn't have kids, but hey, at my age a lot of guys do have kids, so I guess that's something that is negotiable.

I want someone who is romantic and gives me lots of attention; someone who is a big softie at heart and will treat me like a lady – holding doors open etc. Old fashioned style chivalry. A huge thing for me is also someone who can make me laugh, I love to have fun and a wicked sense of humour is definitely a must for me. I can be quite cheeky myself, and I love to take the piss out of someone and get that same banter back. Life is too short to not be able to laugh and find the humour in everything.

I have had so many dick shots sent to me without warning, and let's face it

> *"Hi, I'm only 5ft8 but I guarantee you won't be disappointed"*
>
> *And I guarantee you that I will be…*

"There's a party in my pants and you're invited"

Party for one then...

they aren't pretty things to look at, it just doesn't get me going I'm afraid guys. It's your bedroom skills that are of importance. One of the most awkward experiences that I have probably had whilst internet dating, was with a guy I had been dating for a bit and after a few drinks one night we ended up in bed – note to self, a few drinks is probably not ideal when sleeping with someone for the first time. Men can get a bit droopy and I get that, but this guy just wanted me to keep trying. For hours! To which nothing worked. Nothing! I tried every trick in the book, before finally saying, "I give up tonight, I don't think he wants to play." As if things weren't bad enough already; the next morning was the exact same experience, it was like playing with a lump of playdoh, but you're only able to make various unimpressive chipolata shapes. I think that I switched off after a few hours and started thinking about what I could cook for dinner instead. Maybe not sausages!

Other requirements, I guess would include things like having a good job, their own place would be a bonus, and driving and having their own car would be good as well, because I hate driving. Being able to cook would also help because I can't cook anything, my 13-year-old is a better cook than me, and that's not even an exaggeration.

So, I am fully aware that I have a lot of boxes that I want ticking and it is

"I know I don't look like much now, but I'm growing"

unlikely that I will find my dream man, so instead I'll return back to the real world where I have just been blocked by the guy that had the cheek to blow me off because of a hangover and is clearly pissed off because I didn't want to rearrange our date. X-factor is coming on now though, so I'll open a bottle of wine and maybe have a peek at my inbox. Any dickheads online tonight?

"Your smile is almost as big, warm, and lovely as my penis"

There are so many guys that won't make it into my stories, basically because we had a nice date, but they were also players who were not really willing to give up their single lifestyle. The key to spotting this is how much time they spend logged into their dating account. If you hear the saying, 'Oh, my laptop keeps me logged in all day', don't fall for it. It may stay logged in for 15 minutes or so, but after that it's all them, trust me! One guy even logged in whilst on our first date. I actually caught him over his shoulder as I was returning from the toilet. Suffice to say I didn't see him again!

I think the problem is that men are greedy when it comes to online dating, they get all of these messages and think that the grass is greener; there is always something better out there. So, they keep

"Hey nice lips, what are the other ones like?"

their options open and chat to numerous women whilst they decide who is best. I don't like being

"Oh my, the things I could do to you, meoooowwww"

an option, so I frequently stop conversations with people who are logged in 24/7. Whilst I'm summarising all this as men behaving badly, trust me I've heard that women are just as bad for sending nude pictures and offering sexual favours as well. I've had a fair few offers too, mind you, £600 to go to a hotel for the evening; do I want to star in an adult film; how about being someone's bit on the side for an allowance each month. Shoe fetishes seem to be popular too, I have had lots of stranger requests from guys who seem to be obsessed with feet and shoes.

A lot of people have asked me why I still bother when I have had a lot of knock backs and disappointments, and I guess it's because I'm a hopeless romantic at heart. I believe there is someone out there for everyone. You just have to find them. Well, I have certainly put in my fair share of time and effort, so I reckon I'm owed some good luck soon. I've kissed more than enough frogs, they're slimy and I'm sick of it, but I'm a glad half full kind of girl, so I'll just keep plugging away – my time will come. Plus, I do have lots of spare time, and despite all of my horror stories I do actually enjoy dating and meeting new people. I find it interesting to learn

"Hey gorgeous, fancy a toyboy?"

I've got things in my fridge older than you!

about someone's life and hear the stories they have to tell. Anyone going on a date with me should be forewarned that they may end up being written about. I can't decide whether I would rather be one of the boring and unforgettable ones, or one of the bat shit crazy ones. I think I'll settle for somewhere in the middle, I guess. If you've never tried internet dating but you do want to give it a go, it's probably best to stop reading now, it will put you off trust me; I've had some strange, weird, and scary experiences. That's not to say that I haven't had a few good ones too, you just have to fish around a lot and hope that you hook a good one, instead of a rotting and stinking one. I do tend to take all of the messages with a pinch of salt though, and unfortunately the more of the bad experiences you have online the more likely you are to have prejudices when it comes to the next person. It's a shame because I know there are normal people out there, I'm normal-ish after all! I think my mum only dropped me on my head once as a baby and I'm completely fine!

*"Want to come round...
I'm in bed lonely"*

Does it sound arrogant to call myself a catch? Probably, but I am, and I deserve to find my prince, not a twat in tin foil. I'm determined to find him, so for now I'll keep trudging through the messages...

*"My god, the fun I could
have with you...."*

SO WHAT HAVE I LEARNT FROM ALL MY DATING EXPERIENCES?

I think every date I have been on has taught me something different about the sort of person I am. It almost puts your personality in the spotlight when you are meeting new people. I've screwed up no doubt, I'm not perfect. I've made mistakes but I have definitely learnt from them. I know that I rush into things; I go a million miles per hour, but I have learnt life is a marathon not a sprint. Some of the relationships have definitely gone too fast and have failed because of that, so as much as I am excited when I meet someone I like, I also often feel like there is someone sitting on my shoulder, and normally also my mum's voice in my head, saying "Samantha, slow down and take it easy." So, I try to do exactly that and sometimes it works.

I think in the early days following the painful split from my ex I certainly wasn't ready for dating. I'm an emotional person anyway but I think when

"Ok so a mad question, would you consider dating a guy who was a submissive, you're the boss, I do as you say, total control over me?"

you have someone new offering you a shoulder to cry on… well let's just say they ended up with a soggy shoulder. There's nothing quite like that to make a man run a mile, I can assure you.

"Good morning my future wife. Are you in business?"

Every date or relationship I have had has, I believe, given me something that I can take away from it and as a result I have improved myself. I try to be more laid back and not expect too much. I've learnt to keep my shit to myself, it's not something you want to burden a new relationship with. Further down the line I certainly hope I can share my problems with a partner, but for now I'll keep the conversation we have, and the time spent together happy and fun. That's what dating should be, it's a fun time to laugh and enjoy discovering what makes the other person tick, it's not time to be spent dwelling on the past and what went wrong. I think I've also learnt that there are a lot of moody men in the world! Honestly, I'm starting to think that PMT is not confined to just women. I can't count the number of times that I've had to deal with stroppy tantrums and hissy fits from men. What is it with men who just can't talk or deal with their issues? Instead, they seem to want to throw their toys out of the pram or run and hide. I'm a bit of a fixer I've discovered. I like things to be all good, and if they aren't then I want to put them right. Sometimes you can, but only if there are two

" We will be friends yes, then get to know each other if you like?"

of you working at it. So, sometimes you just have to walk away, which I must admit makes me sad. I hate giving up or failing at anything in life.

MY DATING RULES

So, after months of learning from my own dating experiences, I have now set myself a few dating rules. Aside from the obvious: meet in a busy place and let someone know where you are and who you are with. One problem I have found though, is that I keep going to the same bars. The staff do tend to look at me like I'm a hooker when I turn up with a different date each week. And not only that, I also have a few set dating outfits that I tend to stick to. Same outfit, different man. Note to self… I need to find some new meeting places!

Anyway, I also stick to the no in-house dating until reaching date 5, as a rule. My mum actually came up with this one, so I thought if my mum can do it then so can I! It is so easy to get carried away when you're having a date at home (yours or theirs), and we all know that it's not a good idea to get carried away on the first date. You can pretty much guarantee you won't see them again. Anyone who is worth it will stick around and do some actual dating first, and if they are after nothing more than a quick bunk up,

"My Christ!"

> *"I really want to meet and greet over coffee or lunch one day, then take you home and have mad crazy sex like two rabbits meeting for the first time"*

then they won't. Another rule I like to follow, is to not get pissed on the first date. It's not a good look. See AUSSIE DRUNK story further down – I rest my case. Always do a bit of research beforehand as well, if their pictures seem too good to be true, they probably are. Male models don't need to go on internet dating sites, see I'M A MALE MODEL. I can't believe I fell for that ones, especially as I watch the bloody programme Catfish all of the time! As you get older another rule comes into place as well, don't waste your time on people aren't worth it. I tend to put a lot of effort into relationships, and if they don't do the same then I find that it's best to just move on and find someone who is worth the effort. Life is too short to be chasing people who aren't worth your time. Plenty of fish, and all that! Another rule I have in place is to not talk about your ex on a date… it's just cringe. I don't eat when I'm on a first date either, you're setting yourself up to get stuck on that date for longer than you may want to be there if you do. And if you don't like them and they insist on paying for dinner, then you end up getting accused of using them for a free meal. It's also advisable to always try and see more pictures of someone that aren't just the ones of their dating profile. Preferably a few different ones, not just ones of their face. Many people seem to think that by not showing their body type in their photos, that you won't notice that they are

considerably overweight when you actually meet them.
I've also learnt that you shouldn't take online dating too seriously, if you think that you are going to meet the love of your life – well it's certainly a possibility but it's also unlikely. I guess cupids' arrow does strike occasionally but more often than not all you will receive is a swift kick up the butt.
It sounds awful and it also goes against who I really am, but don't trust anyone. They can hide behind their computer and be who they want to be, or who they want you to think they are. I think some people use it as an alter ego to give themselves a boost, at the expense of other people. It's very easy for people to create a pretend life rather than living the one that they actually have.
I do believe the saying: men are from Mars women are from Venus. I mean men are just so complicated. They want a relationship, then they don't want the commitment that comes with it; then they want commitment but before you know it, it's too much and they're running away; they apparently don't like arguing, but they aren't willing to talk things through and discuss things, and often they just bury their head in the sand with their arse in the air ready to kick. They love the idea of being with someone, but most of the time they are too selfish to really let anyone in. They want a girlfriend but that means thinking of someone else which, again, is something that they aren't willing to do. They are looking for The One, but in the meantime, they want to have them all. They talk the talk but more often than not they can't walk the walk. They claim that they are gentlemen, but they also don't know their arse from their elbow when it comes to

treating a lady right. Most men don't even know what they want, so how can we ever be expected to figure them out?

"R u real?"

MODERN DAY DATING TERMS

Just a few of the modern-day sayings that I have picked up and also have sometimes experienced along the way. Some are pretty harmless, but be warned, some of them are pretty sinister and can potentially be quite damaging.

GHOSTING:
You have a great date, you text back and forth, then one day they just disappear off the face of the planet. You get no closure and you're left wandering what it is you did wrong.

CATFISHING
When someone completely lies about who they really are, they could use someone else's photos to trick you into talking to them. They will come up with an elaborate story about a high-flying modelling career, or this big house they own. Normally ends badly.

HATFISHING

In order to hide their hair – or lack of – they wear a hat in every picture that's on their online dating profile.

KITTENFISHING

Similar to catfishing, but they loosely base their profile on themselves. There may be some truth to it but equally their photos may be very out of date or only vaguely resemble them. Not necessarily lying them, more like stretching the truth.

BREADCRUMBING

Unlike ghosting and disappearing completely, this person will instead continue to send the occasional message with no intention of actually meeting up. They leave the door open to keep you dangling. This could go on for months, or even years. Your left wandering if the person was ever really interested or if they were just wasting your time.

BENCHING

Similar to breadcrumbing, but it is more obvious that they are pursuing other options and you are essentially nothing more than their backup plan.

STASHING

They hide you away and pretend that you don't exist to their friends and family. Every time you post of social media and tag them, they will remove themselves. They claim to like their privacy, but they are actually "stashing" you in the cupboard just in case someone notices you.

"I will be your servant, I will do anything you want, you are stunning"

FIREDOORING

The other person has all the power. They will text you but fail to respond when you text them back. They never make plans to see you, but they expect you to drop everything on the odd occasion they are free. As the name suggests, you can get out, but you can't get back in again. It never allows anyone to enter.

SUBMARINING

This is when someone finishes with you, or ghosts you, then just pops back into your life after having no contact for months, as though nothing happened. They expect you to be completely fine with the fact they have been ignoring you.

CUSHIONING

Staying in contact with one or more people in case things don't go smoothly with your main conquest.

LOVE BOMBING

The new person in your life shows you extreme interest and overwhelming affection. You feel like you've hit the jackpot, they seem perfect. However, once you're in too deep and you have feelings for that person, the love bomber withdraws, and the ugly side of their personality begins to show. You're left in a relationship that is draining and toxic.

HAUNTING

When you think you have finished things with someone and then you notice signs of them lurking on your social media feeds. Randomly liking old pictures etc. Often the notifications are likely to be a deliberate attempt to remind you that they exist and are still around.

PIEHUNTING

"The hunter" deliberately dates heartbroken, vulnerable people who have messy dating histories, or those who've been through a recent break up, as they appear to be grateful for the attention, they are then seen as an easy target. This person exploits people when they are at their lowest.

SLOW FADE

Gradually reducing contact and text response times with a person. Messages and phone calls will gradually taper off. Letting someone down gently, without actually saying that you're calling it a day.

"Are your boobs real?"

[illegible] period. However, once you [illegible] and [illegible]

[illegible]

[illegible]

[illegible]

[illegible]

[illegible]

[illegible]

[illegible]

[illegible] people

[illegible] those who [illegible]

[illegible] appear to be [illegible]

[illegible] The person [illegible]

[illegible]

[illegible]

Our [illegible] and fast response times with a

person [illegible] messages and phone calls will gradually taper off. Letting

[illegible] without actually saying that you're calling it

a day.

[illegible]

MY DATING STORIES

"Wow, wow, wow, its a pity. You tick my boxes too, what shite. Anyway you stay has sweet has you or xxx nicccce"

Right, so you cannot just skip to the end and see if I found the man of my dreams, you'd miss out on all the juicy dating stories that got me to my final destination. As I write this, even I don't know the end result. Maybe I gave up on men and became a lesbian?

So, anyway, if you are still interested in hearing about some of the dates I have been on, here are a few of my dating horror stories, make sure you have a cushion handy…

These are just a small selection of some of my experiences over the last 6 months. Yes, only 6 months, I plan to keep writing until my journey ends and I meet my prince. I'm hoping that by next summer when my year is complete that I will have myself a handsome plus one for my friend's wedding in Jamaica. We can all live in hope…

"Hi Samantha, are you friendly?"

Erm, I'm not a pet dog??!?!

"Do you have nice feet? I like feet"

THE SWINGER

So, this was my first date, and despite how nervous I was it went surprisingly well. He was a nice-looking guy, a bit like a bouncer but I kind of like that. We had good banter and a good laugh, and although there wasn't a kiss at the end, I felt that it went well. So, I waited for the text to ask me out again and as expected it came. Unfortunately, the offer was not quite what I was expecting.

He said that he'd love to see me again and suggested that he take me to one of his favourite places, he then said that he would send me the link. When the link came through it sent me directly to a boudoir site. He explained that it was somewhere that he liked to go, and he would love to share me around!

Now I'm openminded, BUT! I don't share food, never mind men. I had to ask him: did he take one look at me and think, she looks like the type, bet she'll be right up for it. Did I have that sort of face? Despite me not being interested I had to admit that I was slightly fascinated. I questioned him for days as I had never met a real-life 'weirdo' before. I found out a lot that week. Last I heard he had two girls on the go, each unaware of the other, and he was planning to have a little get together.

"Hi, you are beautiful, I have to ask this and please reply. Would you stand or walk on a man for fun, gifts or money?"

THE STALKER

So, this guy starts off ok. Nice guy and he seems like a laugh, I just wasn't sure there was a spark as such. I didn't really fancy him, but we left things on good terms and continued talking for months.

"Hello, is it me you're looking for?"

Then proceeds to quote a whole entire song to me....
with little pictures and emojis.
You could'nt make this shit up.

We kind of became friends and despite me making it clear that I didn't want to date him he still kept offering to fly me off to various locations. All of which I declined as I felt he wanted more. Friends with benefits also kept being suggested, which I also made clear was not going to happen. So, anyway, the chatting continued and eventually I had a spare day and suggested we meet for lunch. NOTHING MORE. So, I drove over to meet him, which was about an hour away, greatly anticipating a nice chat, some lunch, and a catch up.

On arrival he held my hand and I immediately realised that I was letting myself in for more than I bargained for. We chatted over a drink and then he suggested that we go for food. Not asking what I fancied he then

"I like sport, what sport would you challnge me to?"

Oh, I've got this one! A running race. Run really fast in opposite direction and don't come back!

proceeded to look for a Buy One Get One Free offer and whisked me off to a restaurant for a bargain lunch. Don't get me wrong I love a bargain but maybe not the best option for a first date. On the way to the restaurant, he also tried to kiss me, and I was beginning to feel extremely awkward.

"You've got nice tits, but what color are your nipples?"

So, here's my dilemma, I'm bloody hungry and I didn't come all this way to get some horrible slimy tongue thrust down my throat without being at least rewarded with lunch. So, yes, I continued the date but only because I felt I deserved lunch. An hour later and our lunch came to £17 because mine was essentially free. So, when the bill arrived, he looked at me expecting me to put in half, which in any normal circumstance I of course wouldn't mind, not a problem, I always like to pay my way. But I thought for £8.50 and a hellishly slobbery kiss, I'd just let him pick up the bill.

After lunch we walked back through town and he tried to drag me into a park, no doubt for more disgustingly bad kisses. I instead made me excuses and left, only to get a text on the way home telling me we should get a hotel room. At which point I think I may have been sick in my mouth a little bit!

I arrived home and received a text asking if I had liked the

"Can you be descreet?"

Let me discuss it with your wife, I'll get back to you!

"The last time I saw that many tattoos was in a horror movie, can I hire you for Halloween?"

Blocked.

kisses, to which I replied that I hadn't really because I didn't come for that; it was just meant to be friends meeting up. That's when the abuse started, and it still continues to this day. Random nasty text messages, new profiles in my inbox telling me I have a face like a horse and no wonder I'm still single. I'm a fake and that I am just after a free lunch, of all things! Tight git didn't pay for my lunch anyway.

<u>WHIRLWIND THEN GHOST</u>

So, I didn't know what ghosting meant in the dating world until fairly recently. And yes, I have been ghosted, so I can add that to my list. Also, a love bomber is the extreme form of someone ghosting you.

This guy, I have to say, literally blew me away; he was gorgeous. We had been chatting for about a week and then he went on holiday to Spain and suggested I fly out to meet him as a joke, I don't think either of us expected me to be on a plane 3 days later. It just felt right – crazy and spontaneous, yes - but I felt a connection with this guy that I had never felt before. It was love at first sight. He became my everything so quickly, way too quickly actually. We fell in love and spent 4 amazing weeks together. I thought

*"How can I get a date with you? I can send c*ck shot?"*

"Can you watch me wank?"

I had found the love of my life. We made plans for the future and we have even talked about living together and getting married one day. I thought I was in heaven. Everyone around me told me to slow down but I didn't want to, I was loving how intense and crazy it was. He was way too full on and I got sucked in. He'd put me into his phone under 'future wife', we talked about how well our kids would get on, and he even mentioned moving in with me. I told him to slow down, but he seemed to want it all, and soon.

Unfortunately, my perfect man soon showed that he had a very moody side which rang alarm bells and following a weekend together he just got on a train and disappeared out of my life forever. He never spoke to me again; no texts, I was blocked on all communication. To not even have any closure was really hard to deal with. Looking back, it was a crazy time in my life but when you're on that rollercoaster it can be thrilling and exciting. So, I went from one day planning a life with someone, and then the next day that person is gone forever, without so much as a goodbye. I had been ghosted…

MALE MODEL

"Excuse my forwardness, I'd love to slide my tongue up your arse, I bet you taste as good as you look"

So, this one still shocks me to this day. It was the most bizarre experience and it certainly made me more cautious when talking to people. Like something straight out of the programme Catfish, I got caught. Male model, gorgeous, fit, tall, loads of hot photos, totally believable story. I thought I'd hit the jackpot. Looking back now it's ridiculous but at the time this guy really had the whole story going on. Even to the point where I asked him to send a photo of himself now, so he did. It all looked genuine. The thing that made it so believable was that he spent hours on the phone to me for a whole week. And I mean hours. Literally some days he would phone me 20 times a day. I like a lot of attention don't get me wrong, but even I was thinking that it was a bit much.

> *"Do you prefer length or girth?"*

Anyway, we arranged to meet at a local pub on a Sunday. He was going to drive all the way from Birmingham to meet me. I thought, wow this guy is putting in the effort. I did question his whole modelling thing and even said to him a few times: "how do I know you are who you say you are?" But he seemed so confident and even said that "you'll see on Sunday, why would I waste this much time if I wasn't real?"

Everyone around me was dubious, they all questioned the finer details that weren't quite adding up; the fuzzy photos, the broken camera so that he couldn't video call me etc. But he'd sucked me in by this point, he had managed to convince me that he

> *"Fancy a 9 inch"?*
>
> *Don't think they do that at Subway do they?*

was the guy in the photos. Luckily on the Saturday before I went to a friend's house for drinks and her sister-in-law was a real investigator type. She suggested we do some research and see what we could find out about this guy. Us women are good at investigating, trust me! Bingo, within minutes she had found an American actors' website where all of his photos had come from.

"Love your milkshakes!"

So, we started to have a bit of fun with him. We put him on loud-speaker and started to flirt and tell him that we would video call him from bed soon. I actually wanted to see who would turn up on the Sunday as he was so adamant that he would. Some sad, ugly pervert probably. He started to get suspicious though, so we had to call him out on the American actor website before he blocked us, I wanted to have the satisfaction on making sure he knew that we were aware he wasn't real. But, of course, once he got caught out, he blocked me immediately. But I still wander to this day, what was the motivation? I'm guessing that he had no job and life and took pleasure in wasting other people's time. Either that or he was hoping to get some sexy pictures, who knows. I'll never understand that one, but it certainly did make me doubt people's photos from then on. If they look like a model, then it's probably not really them.

"May I pleasure you with my tongue?"

CROYDON GEEZER

"Longing to hear from you... From India..."

When I go on a date, I do like to put a bit of effort in; I always look nice, hair done, makeup – nice jeans and a blazer maybe. You know that when your date rocks up in dazzling white trainers, wearing shades indoors and a fake limp and says 'alright babes', that it's not going to go well. I didn't even understand the language this guy was talking. Maybe it's my age, but if he was talking English it certainly didn't make any sense to me. We were worlds apart. That still didn't stop him from trying to slip his arm around my shoulder in a snake like move though. If I didn't have killer heels on that day, then I think I would have run straight back to my car.

MAN MOUNTAIN

So, this one did look promising, I must say. Huge mountain of a guy. Mum saw his picture and said he looked like brick shit house but as the kids were in earshot, she actually called him a shed. 6ft5 and a big heart; he sounded amazing. And to be fair from the minute we met we did hit it off and we quickly started dating. He described himself as the softest most laid-back guy going, and I genuinely thought he was. We spent a few weeks together and it was all going well until I happened to mention that it must be hard doing shift work and how much it must have affected his dating life. He did lots of random nights shifts and it was hard fitting in dating, but it was ok, I was happy to

"Can I dominate you?"

figure it out. But following my comment Mr Laid Back disappeared very quickly and in his place Mr Stroppy appeared. He ranted and raved about his job hours and how he was always getting grief over it, how his job comes first, and he'll never let a woman control him blah blah blah!

> *"Hi. I'm horny"*
>
> *Unusual name...*

Wow, well when you have chilled out and stopped losing your shit Mr Cool, I'll be washing my hair. We never spoke again.

RAT FACE

Very simple, nice guy, going ok until he laughed and pulled his weird face that made him look like a rat. Put me right off.

STRAIGHT OUTTA GOONIES

Now this guy was lovely, don't get me wrong, but he did resemble the monster guy from the Goonies, 6ft8 with a face that looked like it had been through a food processor. But you have to give these guys a chance, I guess I was hoping that his personality and height would distract from his face. I was wrong.

MISERABLE ORANGE JUMPER MAN

Now this guy seemed pretty funny on the phone, very witty and I enjoyed chatting to him.

So, I went to meet him, once again driving further than I

> *"You look familiar, have we had sex before?"*

should have but I thought why not. On my arrival I was met with the most miserable faced bastard I had ever encountered. He didn't smile when he was greeting me, he looked like he had the world on his shoulders and he generally made me feel like I wanted to jump off the nearest bridge! I kept asking if he was ok, and he said he was fine, but his face was definitely saying differently. And to top it all off, his dress sense was horrendous, the orange old man jumper he was wearing looked like something out of a horror movie. The final straw then came when he tried to kiss me, it's safe to say that I made a swift exit and drove as fast as I could to get away.

"I am a musical lawyer, and I will serenade you on my baby grand.
Unless you want to skip to the bedroom?"

AUSSIE DRUNK

Well, we all know the Australians like to drink. I just didn't realise quite how much until this guy came along. We met in London, and I guess a clue would have been the text from the train telling me that he was already pretty drunk. Great. Shoot me now. Anyway, we met at a pub and the first drink he ordered was a double tequila slammer. This guy was hardcore. To be fair it was a Saturday, and he did say that he only drank one night a week, so I thought

"You're fit"

Inventive! Imagine the interesting and deep conversations we could have!

fair enough. I can handle my drink, so I had a few and tried to keep up.

We went on a bit of a pub crawl and it was a laugh, and although I was a little bit merry by this point, it is safe to say that he had surpassed that stage and was very drunk. We finally settled at a riverside bar and whilst he propped up the bar slurring his speech, I sat and chatted to a couple of the bar workers. They couldn't believe that he had got in such a state on our first date. We all laughed about it, but I also knew that it was probably best for me to get myself home.

The next day I texted him and asked how he was feeling. His reply was: "pretty hungover, can't remember anything past the first half hour." Wow, a whole date missing, what was the point! Then within minutes his attitude completely changed, and he started being really off with me. By this point I was confused, and I was questioning what it is that was causing him a problem. He then proceeded to tell me that I had somehow managed to steal his bank details and pay for my Uber home, costing him £50! The moron had used his card all over London and didn't recognise the transactions he had made. Blocked!

<u>TEE TOTAL</u>

I only managed the one date with this guy. When you get a text after

"You're gorgeous, and hot, and way too good for me, I'd never get with anyone like you, not even in my wildest dreams, if I did though you'd make me the happiest man alive, oh god, to have you as my girlfriend, I'd never let you go, I'd never let you out of my sight, I'd be with you forever holding you tight and watching you sleep..."

Well you're not my worst nightmare!

a date saying "I think we have a problem, I don't drink, and you seem to drink quite a lot" you just know that it isn't going to work out. Pass me a large vodka!

"Is 5ft11 short? Jeez!"

MY EX, MY EX, MY EX

Major rule of dating: DON'T TALK ABOUT YOUR EX! God, this guy did not shut up about his ex and her new boyfriend, and what it was that they were doing to piss him off, and how he was over her, but she still managed to get to him, and what they did to piss him off last week, and how she's under his skin but he'd over her, and how she makes him jealous, blah fucking blah. Two hours I had to listen to this shit. I couldn't even get a word in edgeways to tell him the date was over.

TICKET TO THAILAND

Why go on a dating site if you are planning on spending at least half of the year in Thailand? Why would you not mention something like that on your profile? I know some people could possibly tag along, but not me I'm a mum of two. Yet another few weeks wasted on someone.

"Hi,nice profile, fancy a chat?"
"Hello, you there"
"I don't bite"
"Hi, I'm still waiting for a hi back"
"Are you going to talk to me or not?"

Blocked

ONE ARMED BANDIT

"Hi. You'll do."

Oh, such charm!

Most of us, I imagine, would have the common sense to think that going on a first date with a broken arm whilst drugged up to the eyeballs on painkillers, would probably not be the best of ideas, and that it would probably be best to rearrange. First impressions and all that? Well, this guy seemingly didn't realise that, as he turned up to the date off his tits on medication. I mean he was all over the place, and he was so random in his conversations and his behaviour was completely bizarre. When he left in his car, he even drove up the wrong side of the road.

To be fair I did see him again when he wasn't on medication, and he was quite random and amusing and he was also kind of fun to be around. But a total bad boy; definitely not boyfriend material. I have this habit of picking the people that are bad for me. They all look the same, toned, tattooed, and have normally been to prison!

"I've got big shoes."

OLD RAVER

Well, this one didn't even make it as far as a date. After adding him on WhatsApp and seeing his profile picture, I questioned what the deal was with the cap he was wearing sideways and at his age, in a joking way of course! I was expecting him to say that it was fancy dress outfit or something. Apparently, it was his raving hat. Blocked!

2ND DATE WITHOUT MEANING TO,
7 YEARS ON

*"Here's an idea, I'll come round to yours with a bottle of wine and we can get f*cked up?"*

Erm, let me think about it whilst I dial 999!

So, I was chatting to a friend and all the while this guy keeps texting me. My friend said "Oh, he's keen" and I reply about him just being some guy from a small village near me. To which my friend then replied: "I was chatting to a guy from there too, he was really keen, kept texting." Hmm, a strange coincidence maybe?

So yes, it turned out we had both been chatting to the same guy, although not at the same time. My friend decided that I needed to go on a date with him to see what he was like – thanks chick, I'll take one for the team then!

I wasn't too sure from looking at some of his pictures, he looked a bit rough, but to put curiosity at bay I went anyway and met him in the pub. He had, after all, reassured me that it didn't matter if I didn't fancy him as loads of women think he's hot. He can't be that bad then, surely? As soon as I walked in, I realised that from the back he was a lot larger than his pictures let on and he was wearing baggy large man jeans held up with an ill-fitting belt which looked awful. The worst was still yet to come. He was massively balding, something that was not shown in his photos, and

"Are those things real?"

then as he turned around, I also realised that I had already been on and unsuccessful date with him, 7 years ago! He was butt ugly then, now he was butt ugly and a lot older. He didn't remember me, so we debated over a drink whether we had or hadn't met previously, before I decided that it was time to make a swift exit. As per the date 7 years prior, he texted me afterwards to tell me that he had a lovely time, and we should do it again. Yeah, catch you in another 7 years maybe. Or not!

> *"Here's a picture of my fireplace. And my dog. And my co*k"*

CANT MEET - WONT MEET?

I can't even explain this one to this day. This guy seemed like he was very interested, very into me, like he fancied me. But twice we arranged dates and he either didn't show or he just went off the radar.

After asking him if he was in prison, married, really a woman... I realised at that point: actually, did it even matter? He was just another time waster with no real intentions of meeting. I honestly think a lot of people go on there just to pass the time, they come up with an alter ego and message people just to fill some time in their sad little lives. Maybe they are actually married and they're loving a bit of extra attention? Who knows? But be aware, 30% of the men on dating sites are in fact married men. Scary, eh!

MUMMYS BOY

"How are you still single, what's wrong with you?"

So, this little romance lasted a few weeks. Essentially it was all going well until I kind of got ghosted again. He just disappeared with nothing more than a text saying, "work sending me to Scotland. Be in touch." One week later he finally comes crawling back into my life and admits he'd lied about having his own place and when I had invited myself round one night he had freaked out. The Scotland thing was also made up, and would I give him another chance… Erm, in the words of Simon Cowell, that would be a big fat no!

HUNCHBACK WITH A SHIT TATTOO

So, I've now learnt my lesson – if people only show headshots then there is normally a reason for that. After chatting to, and arranging a date with this guy, he then proceeded to tell me that he was not in as good a shape as he used to be. Tell me after we've arranged a date why don't you! Feeling bad and not wanting to let him down, I went on the date anyway. Needless to say, as soon as I stepped out of the car, I thought 'oh shit'. He was not my type at all, he seemed like a bit of a hunchback because he had bad posture and a beer belly to add to

"You need to get your tattoos lasered off and your teeth fixed. You're so desperate"

Blocked!

it. God. How am I going to get out of this one? So, we chatted away and there was no spark there, whatsoever. We then got onto the subject of tattoos and I mentioned that I liked nice tattoos on guys. He then proceeded to tell me that he had an amazing one, but upon lifting his sleeve to show me his tattoo it could only be described as something that resembled the cheap football stickers my 8-year-old son collects. That was it, game over. He said something along the lines of when he'd been on dates in the past and there was no spark, that he wouldn't sit it out, he'd just get up a leave. So, I did exactly that. He was shocked, I think. Must have thought the shit tattoo did it for me!

> *"Are you really a man?"*
>
> *Are you?*

HARLEY PLAYER

No, this is not some American sports player, this was a guy that happened to ride a Harley and was a player. Essentially, he seemed perfect. Lovely looking, genuine and looking for a relationship. Our first date went as expected, chemistry, flirting, and a nice kiss at the end. I drove home with a

> *"Have sex with me and I promise never to talk to you again."*
>
> *Deal, although how about we skip straight to the second part where you never talk to me again?*

big smile on my face and arrived home to a text from him saying he was excited to have met me and would love to see me again, he was excited to see where the future went with me blah blah blah. Jackpot, I thought, maybe this is the guy I've been waiting for. My bubble would soon burst though. After arranging a second date, I told him I was hiding my profile online as I was focusing on just him and wanted to see where it went. I wasn't into chatting to multiple people, and if I met someone that I really liked I wasn't the sort to line up other dates. Unfortunately, that's when he came out with a line that still shocks me now: "oh, I'm still window shopping, I like to keep my options open, but don't worry your top of the pile at the moment." There's only one word I can use to describe him… Dick!

HAIRY CHEEK

This one is relatively short. Met in a pub. Sat down to have a drink. Before I'd even managed to start chatting to him, I spotted a long hair on his face. To think that I then tried to swish it away, saying something like oh you have a hair there, only to discover it was a 2-inch-long hair attached to his face. Not knowing how to deal with said hair situation I kind of kept swishing at it, he was asking if it was gone, to which I replied, "Oh yeah I think it has now." Of course, it hadn't. is spent the whole date not being able to concentrate on anything and wandering

"Apart from being sexy, what do you do for a living?"

how long it was, and if he knew it was there but also thinking how mortified I was that I had almost tugged it. Cringe!

"It's not you, it's me, I just can't commit to anyone."

That old chestnut!

SIDE PROFILE GUY

I once made the mistake of chatting to someone for quite some time having only seen one side profile picture of him. I guess I forgot my very basic rule of checking out a few pictures before lining up a date. When I did ask for more pictures, he made various excuses as to why he couldn't send any. "I've got none on this phone." "Will send over later." "Oh, I don't like my photo being taken." I think alarm bells start to ring after a while and you realise that this isn't going to be what you're hoping for, when it does come through. And my gut feeling was right, he was a balding minger and had somehow managed to disguise it using a side profile picture. How then do you politely say, sorry I don't actually fancy you? It's never going to go down well. So, you kind of drop the bombshell and duck for cover. Suffice to say he didn't take it well.

You get all sorts of names; shallow, up your own arse, superficial. If they were just honest from the beginning though, you would see what you were getting straight away. There has to be physical attraction.

SHORTIE

"I would dominate you all night long."

As a rule, I only date men who are over 6ft3.

It means that I can still wear my heels. But on a night out locally, I did bump into someone who I had seen online, and although he was my height whilst I was in heels, I still felt like I towered over him a bit. But we got chatting and I did think he was a really funny and lovely guy. So, I got in touch with him and we arranged a date. In my flat shoes obviously.

So, this is a big thing for me you'll understand. Height is my number one tick box. It means I feel safe and comfortable, and kissing a shorter guy just feels weird to me. But I did want to be openminded and see if I could date a shorter guy. The answer is no. It's just wrong on all levels. Feels like you're out with your son in my opinion. You feel like a freak, and all those heeled shoes that I'd never be able to wear, it's just not worth it. Never, ever again. If you're a tall girl and you're ever tempted to try it, stick some heels on a slap yourself around the face.

BLONDIE TONGUE TICKLER

So, I had just realised at the grand age of 39 that I'd never been on a date with a blond guy! Well, there is a first time for everything, so off I went. This guy was a proper South Londoner, tall, blonde, kind of Scandinavian looking,

"What I lack in height I make up for with girth... does that work for you" although his pictures were a bit blurry, so I did have my reservations.

"You look amazing, are we compatible.. yes or no?"

On arrival he was nice looking, with a nice smile – all good so far. We chatted, had some drinks, and although the conversation wasn't quite as comfortable as I would've liked, we seemed to get on well, a grower maybe? That was until we left the pub and went for a walk along the river. At which point he pounced and thrust his tongue so far down my throat I thought he was trying to retrieve my dinner, and he the proceeded to kiss and lick my neck. Now, I'm no prude and I don't mind a little subtle kiss after a good date, but this guy was quite literally devouring me in public. Taking me back a bit he did say, "sorry did you want me to be more gentlemanly, am I too forward." I was so shocked by the speed of the onslaught that I just stuttered, "erm, maybe" whilst I was really thinking that this would have been a good date to arrange one of those emergency phone calls for. You know the ones "what, oh god really… my son's foot has dropped off and I must leave immediately!" When he then said. "fancy a cuppa?" Which basically means I'd like to take you back to my place and rip your clothes off at record breaking speed, I decided to make a speedy getaway. Funny thing was, he texts me the next afternoon and told me that I wasn't his type!

GIRL, WOMAN, BABE

"Can we get just married and skip all the other bollocks?"

Up until this stage, I should point out that all of my dates have been written from memories, or should I say nightmares! I have now caught up to date and this now current and written more as a diary, on a date-to-date basis.

So, I have now met up with this guy a few times. He has potential. Is he the one to bring my book to an abrupt end? Well, I live in hope, although I'm just not sure right now. He's tall, handsome, has the most amazing bright blue eyes that are simply mesmerising. We get on well, seem to have a lot to chat about and we have a laugh. He's a typical scaffolder and I can just picture him doing the "Oi, Oi, darling!" to random passing women.

Very much a South London lad, and although I'm nowhere near posh, I definitely notice the differences sometimes when we're talking. Although there is also a 'but'; he's only 34 and men can be immature for their age. I've started to notice little things within our conversations that make me notice the age difference. When he talks about driving his car fast or spinning it in the snow, I can't help but thinking 'grow up'. He also swears like a trooper and he smokes, which is something I hate. So, I sometimes find myself trying to change him a bit, which obviously is not a good thing. He's already trying to stop dropping the C bomb in public and cutting down on the cigarettes.

*"F*cu you in your panties."*

And the reason for the title, he has an annoying

"What are you hoping to find on here? I'm hoping to find someone genuine, honest, kind, loving and kinky as there's a few things I'd like to try..."

habit of calling me girl. "Alright girl, how you doing, girl?" Again, this is not sitting well with me, so now every time he says it, he then tries to correct himself. I'm now greeted with, "Hey girl, woman, I mean babe, sorry!" So, he's trying, bless him, but how much should someone have to change the way they naturally are to suit someone else?

So, anyway he has potential, and he is trying hard, a bit like a lost puppy trying to find a new owner. He is lovely though and only time will tell, a few dates really aren't enough time to truly get to know someone. We're spending the weekend together soon, so I guess that will reveal more about how well we actually do get on. If by the end of the weekend I'm sick of the sight of him then my dating experiences and my book will continue. But for now, I've hidden my profile and I'll give the young lad a shot...

4 weeks later...

So, I gave it a shot, but here I am back again. I had hoped that maybe I would get my happy ending and wouldn't be back on the dating scene again, but I guess it's not my time yet.

I've had a fun month, I've done the proper dating thing with him, and whilst it has been lovely to have someone in my life, I soon discovered that he has his flaws; ones that would be harder for me to get past. Him being younger meant that I regularly had to deal with some childish strops over absolutely nothing. Last night I fell asleep snuggled up to him laughing and chatting, and then at midnight I woke up to him sitting in bed with a face like thunder. What did I do? I have no idea, but after a few warnings recently about him growing up and talking to me about whatever it is rather than sulking about it, I ended up finishing things right there and then. It's such a shame, especially as I had got used to having him around, I guess you could say that I am feeling a bit empty this morning. But hey, lesson learnt; men can be immature so date the older ones! I'd also quite enjoyed not being on the dating site, and just being more settled for a little bit, but here I am reluctantly reopening my profile and starting all over again. Not the greatest of prospects, and I'm sure there will be new idiots to deal with that weren't there a month ago!

SHEEP SHAGGER

He wasn't a sheep shagger, obviously, well not to my knowledge, but hey who knows, the internet is full of weirdos, but he was Welsh. So, this date actually went really well, we had such a laugh and spent most of the date discussing why the Welsh had got themselves a name for shagging sheep. We didn't really uncover any reasons, but we had a good laugh regardless. He was lovely looking, drove a 100-mile round trip to see me, a nice kiss at the end of the evening, and a second date arranged. All was going well until I got back home, and I noticed

"Right, so Im not 6ft3, but I can bring cuban heels or maybe even a ladder?"

Yawn!

that he had gone straight back online chatting to other women for hours! I mean, really? Are men all that greedy? They are like kids in a sweet shop I'm sure of it, they can't decide what sweet is best, so they ram the whole god damn lot in their mouth.

"I like my single life, I'm not ready to give it up."

Huh? Why are you on a date then?

NO FILTER

This guy seems perfect. He's been on online dating on and off for years, a bit like me. He wants to settle down and he's looking for something long-term. He's not a player and he's not lining up dates left, right and centre. He's nice looking, tall and funny. He has a beard, but hey, that can be shaved off once I get the chance! He works just around the corner from where I work as well, and we practically pass each other on a daily basis. It would be perfect if it works out; I can't help but think of the possibility of nice lunches and after work drinks.

We meet for a quick lunchtime drink. First impressions, nice looking, a bit skinnier than I like and also a bit geekier, but I can live with that if he's a nice guy. We chat and have a laugh. He's got a very strange deep voice which I can't stop thinking about whilst we're talking. Plus, I keep looking at how narrow his shoulders are. Such a strange thing to put you off, but they are a bit like a child's shoulders. But I'm trying to get over the small issues that aren't really important in the grand scheme of things. So anyway, at the end of our lunchtime drinks he invites me out for dinner after work that evening.

As the evening goes on, I realise that he is brutally honest and doesn't really understand how to make a good impression on a first date. He doesn't have a filter at all and says exactly what is on his mind. Comments like "I've got no friends" and "I kind of use people for a purpose" slip out. Which is funny at first when I am still trying to figure him out, but as the evening goes on, it's safe to say that I was beginning to see why he was still single.

He kept grabbing his stomach and saying, "I'm fat, aren't I?" in a weird under-confident kind of way. He justifies his comments by saying that he's just trying to be himself and he wouldn't want to lie and then further down the line appear to be a dickhead, he said that he'd rather be himself from the beginning. I try and explain that it's like a job interview and you want to be the best version of yourself in order to impress people, but it's falling on deaf ears. He has barely asked any questions about me and while the conversation is easy going, I do feel that although he fancies me, he's not really interested me or in knowing anything about me or my life. I ask loads of questions about him and after a while I begin to realise that this isn't really working out. The nail in the coffin… mid-dinner

I want 3 chances to guess what car you drive just by summing you up so far?

Sure, can I have 1 guess why your still single?

"I normally avoid tall girls; they freak me out. I normally date really short girls, makes me feel more manly." Hmm. I immediately feel very uncomfortable, and whilst he's trying to dig his way out of the hole, I can't order a taxi quick enough! I mean who says that to a 6ft tall girl and actually expects it to go down well. And so, what I thought would be ultra-convenient with us working so close, is now my shopping nightmare instead. He manages the car park where I shop on a daily basis. That's not going to be at all awkward.

Oh well, I'm off on holiday with a girlfriend next week. I wonder what stories that will bring…
So, how will it all end? Did I meet my knight in shining armour, get swept off my feet and live happily ever after?
I guess that's the next part of my story!

MY LIFE AS IT IS NOW.....

Fast forward a few years and I'm back here and writing again but from a completely different perspective this time. I feel that my life has changed so much from how it was a few years ago when I was dating and first dreaming about meeting someone. I had hoped that it would all work out and I would meet someone to settle down with, but I never quite knew if online dating was the route to get me there. My life as it is now, is how it always should have been, but the getting there has definitely been a tough ride.

After all my amusing stories I continued to date, and I met someone who I spent two years with. Unfortunately, it was very toxic relationship, in fact it was actually pretty similar to my previous marriage, annoyingly. I felt I had fallen into the exact same trap again of being tricked into thinking he was a genuinely nice guy, only to discover the "real" person 6 months later. I found myself falling into a really bad habit of picking people who mostly turned out to be someone completely different to who they had

portrayed themselves as.
I spent two years listening to lies and apologies. It nearly broke me, for the second time in my life, I was with someone who quite literally sucked the life out of me emotionally. I kept questioning why this kept happening to me. What had I done to deserve this amount of upset and vile behaviour, that had been coming my way for years?
So, after two long and hard years, I was single once again. I was 41 by this point and I had spent most of my adult life going from one bad relationship to another. Dating over and over in between, each time to no avail.
I decided that it was now time to focus on me, it was time to embrace single life. Enjoy girls' nights out and weekends away. And that's exactly what I did. I was still on that dating sites, but the no longer seemed as appealing to me as they once had.
I guess after all that time the novelty had worn off and maybe I was also losing faith in the quality of men out there. It was the same old rubbish that I had experienced for years. I was losing hope, there's no doubt about it. But equally the thought of being a lonely old cat lady kept me clinging in there. A small but very slight glimmer of hope that after all this time it could possibly work out. I had heard success stories, but the ones that I had heard of were few and far between.

So, real life took over and when I got invited to a Butlin's 80's Revival Weekend I jumped at the chance. Not really knowing what I had to look forward to, I just thought of it as a great chance to let my hair down and have fun with the girls.

I now realise that a lot of people go there for a completely different reason, mainly to party but also for married people to experience the single life whilst their loving spouse is sitting at home unaware of the shag-fest happening elsewhere. It was crazy weekend that's for sure. I danced all weekend until my feet hurt and I barely survived Survival Sunday, aptly named because by then you're hanging out of our arse and the hangover feels like a 10-tonne truck is heading your way.

"Hi, you ok?
Hi
U ok
You OK
HI?"

OMG, yes, I'm ok!

MY HAPPY ENDING

And so, this is where my story twists, in a strange moment of fate. It was 4am on the Monday morning that I was due to drive home from Butlins, and I couldn't sleep. I had a horrendous drive home ahead of me and with a hangover rapidly approaching, I was lying in bed wondering how on earth I was going to make it home alive. Putting off the inevitable drive, I made a cup of tea and logged in to my internet dating profile. I should mention at this point, that online dating in the middle of the night can be a bit odd, to say the least. Most normal people are too busy sleeping at that hour. So, I went to my inbox and there was a message from someone who was also online at that crazy hour. We began chatting and two hours later the conversation was still going. We had a great laugh and I really didn't want to stop the conversation but knowing that I needed to leave to get home, I signed off.

"If God gave me beautiful girl as you, I be loyal to her all life, but gorgeous girls always go for wrong man..."

At this point online dating conversations can abruptly end, as people get busy, talk to other people, drift away etc, never to be seen again.

After driving a very treacherous drive home avoiding random animals on pitch black roads, I finally staggered through my door and collapsed on the sofa. Ping! A message: "I HOPE YOU GOT HOME SAFE, SPEAK SOON XX"

My life progressed into something amazing from there. I did meet my prince! We've been together for 10 months now. His name is David, and he is the best thing that has happened to me. He's supportive, thoughtful, unselfish, and caring. Pretty much everything that I have ever wished for in a person, yet I also always felt that it may not have been possible, and that it wasn't real to find that dream person that you can spend the rest of your life with.

I've realised that all of the superficial rubbish that I used to look for isn't actually important. I was looking for all the wrong things in a person. My boyfriend isn't anything like the ideal man that I described earlier on in this book; he doesn't go to the gym or have tattoos for one. He's handsome in his own unique way, and even more importantly, his biggest quality is his heart and his ability to make me feel like the most important person in the world.
I have friends who have said that they have these amazing relationships and that they never argue with their partners, and before I always doubted whether that was truly possible. I am now experiencing that for myself, and I want to encourage other people to realise their dreams when it comes to finding the right person.

I'm now studying to become a life coach and I hope to be able to share my experiences with others, and hopefully help to encourage other people by doing so. I want other people to be in good, healthy, and supportive relationships that lift them up rather than dragging them down. I have many friend and clients that I know deserve the best; they are good, caring people who keep settling for far less than they deserve.
My life is now going in directions that I never dreamt that it could or would. I wake up every day excited about what's coming next.

I have actually met someone amazing. My Prince Charming. My person. My ride or die. My future husband… maybe. Hopefully. Someone who makes me feel complete. We have some amazing dreams to fulfil together…
So, for now, I will be putting my laptop down and enjoying my real-life relationships. It's been emosh!

UNIQUE DATING IDEAS:

Struggling for some dating ideas? Try mixing it up a bit. Be unique and different. Stand out from the crowd!

1. COOK A RECIPE

Pick a recipe to cook together (or apart if you can't get together). Learning to cook together is great fun. If you can't be together then call each other whilst you're both cooking and then sit and eat together via a video call.

2. CAMPING/GLAMPING

Grab a tent and get away from it all. Or even try backyard camping, it can still fun and romantic. Snuggled together under the stars with a BBQ or small fire.

3. TAKE A DANCE CLASS.

It's not only good fun but means you get to flirt up close and personal and really see if there's a physical connection between you!

4. POWER OUT NIGHT.

No devices or TV. Just candles and romance. Maybe a boardgame or card game and a glass of wine.

5. FOSSIL/TREASURE HUNTING

Beach walks can be so romantic. Do some research on your local area. There are some places it can actually be really easy to find fossils. Look up finding fossils in your area and see where the best places are to look. Or invest in a cheap metal detector. A great way to get some fresh air, exercise and have some fun.

6. BREWERY OR FACTORY TOUR.

Can be pretty interesting and you get some from free tasters!

7. GO KARTING

An exhilarating date that can also bring out your competitive side in a fun way.

8 YOGA/FITNESS CLASS

Maybe a date more suitable for when you know each other a little better.

9. ROCK CLIMBING

Bet they haven't done that before on a date! Not for everyone.

10. BOTANICAL GARDENS

A quiet peaceful place you can wander and get to know each other.

11. COMEDY STORE

Maybe best suited for a date further down the line, but at least you'd laugh and have fun.

12. WATCH A SUNSET.

It doesn't get much more romantic. Take a picnic and a blanket.

13. ICE SKATING

You'll both either be really good or really bad, but it is fun finding out. See if they help you up when you fall over or if they will laugh at your expense!

14. HIT THE COUNTRYSIDE AND TAKE SCENIC PHOTOS

You can always pick up some tips online. Get of the beaten track and head for some local beauty spots.

15. TENNIS

See if you can remember how to play or just run around like silly buggers.

16. GO FOR A RUN

Even if you're not that into fitness, give it a go, and you will be able to encourage each other to do more than you would alone.

17. REVISIT YOUR FIRST DATE PLACE

Take a walk down memory lane and reminisce on all the details from your first date.

18. CREATE A TIME CAPSULE

Put in all your favourite memories together. Bury it or hide it to be rediscovered one day in the future.

19. LEARN MEDITATION OR MINDFULNESS TOGETHER

A great way to de-stress, reassess life and chill out together

20. AFTERNOON TEA

Who doesn't love a huge tower of cakes and sandwiches!

MOST IMPORTANTLY, HAVE FUN!

GETTING TO KNOW SOMEONE

We used these random questions to keep the connection in-between dates. It's a great way to get to know someone from afar. Questions you may not be brave enough to ask in person, but over text or email…

1. What is your guilty pleasure?
2. How many times have you been in love?
3. What makes you weird?
4. What is your biggest pet hate?
5. Give me a pet name that only you can call me?
6. What are you saving money for as a treat for yourself?
7. What job did you want to do as a child?
8. Have you ever been skinny dipping?
9. What's your favourite part of my body?
10. If you could go anywhere in the world right now where would
you go?
11. Are you a clean or messy person?

12. What's one thing you love and one thing you hate about yourself?
13. If you could change one thing in your life right now, then what would it be and why?
14. What's the stupidest thing you've done because someone dared you?
15. If you could trade lives with someone who would it be?
16. What's one thing I don't know about you?
17. What's your favourite film?
18. What are you most likely to stay up all night talking about?
19. What is something that you wish you'd accomplished in life by now?
20 What are you most looking forward to in the next 10 years?
21. What's the most interesting thing you've seen online this week?
22. Have you ever cried at a movie?
23. Which products would you stockpile if you found out they weren't going to be producing anymore?
24. Describe your life using one word?
25. If your food is bad at a restaurant, do you complain?
26. When things break do you prefer to fix them or replace them?
27. In what situation, or place, would you feel most uncomfortable in?
28. What's something you've tried that you would never ever try again?
29. What do you wear in bed?
30 Are you scared of anything?

31. What is the best and worst part of your personality?
32. Use an emoji to flirt with me?
33. What did you think when you first saw me?
34. What's your biggest turn on?
35. What's your biggest turn off?
36. What are your deal-breakers?
37. Would you rather be called sexy or smart?
38. Who's your celebrity crush?
39. What makes you nervous?
40. What's the best gift you have ever received from someone?
41. Big spoon or little spoon?
42. If animals could talk which would be the rudest?
43. What would you do if I kissed you right now?
44. Do you believe in love at first sight?
45. If you were arrested what would your friends and family assume it is that you'd done?
46. What two items could you buy that would make the cashier most uncomfortable?
47. If you were an animal, what would you be?
48. What do you find attractive in a potential partner?
49. What's your all-time favourite memory?
50. What's one thing you want to achieve before you die?
51. Do you have a secret fantasy?
52. What are your earliest memories?
53. Would you rather go out on a Saturday night or stay in?
54. What's the sexiest item of clothing you could put on right now?

55. Have you ever been accidentally caught naked?

56. If you were to win the lottery what would be the first three things you would buy?

57. What's the one thing that totally chills you out when you're stressed?

58. Have you ever been arrested?

59. Have you ever taken the blame for something you didn't do?

60. Do you have a secret talent?

61. What drink have your drunk so much of that the thought of it now makes you feel sick?

62. Who is the craziest person you know and why?

63. How long does it take you to get ready to go out?

64. Which celebrity, dead or alive, would you like to have dinner with?

65. What would your mum say about you right now?

66. If you could pick a new first name what would it be?

67. Would you rather explore space or the ocean?

68. If you got stuck on a desert island, name one person who you would want there and one you wouldn't?

69. What's the weirdest thing you have seen in someone else's home?

70. Name 3 things you'd take to a desert island.

71. Would you rather hear the good news or bad news first?

72. What was your favourite toy growing up?

73. What would you do if you were invisible for the day?

74. What's your favourite smell in the whole world?

75. Are you concerned with what other people think about you?

76. What's the best piece of advice you've received?
77. What's the stupidest way you have hurt yourself?
78. If you were a fly on the wall, where would you land?
79. What's your favourite sex position?
80. What's the worst date you have ever been on?
81. If you had to flee the country, where would you go?
82. Have you ever had or wanted plastic surgery?
83. How lucky are you and why?
84. What super-power do you wish you had?
85. What skill do you wish you had?
86. What's the strangest thing you've ever eaten?
87. What's the worst job you've ever had?
88. If you were king or queen for the day, what would be your first new rule?
89. Who is the most famous person you have ever met?
90. What's your least favourite take away?
91. Do you have any scars and how did you get them?
92. Have you ever saved someone's life?
93. What piece of advice would you offer to your younger self?
94. Who would you hate to see naked?
95. Have you ever had a stalker?
96. Would you rather be Batman or Spider-Man?

*"Happily ever after
is not a fairytale,
it's a choice"*

About the Author

Samatha Thorne lives in Dartfortd, Kent.
Shes 42 years old and is also a Beautician and Graphic Designer.
Shes lives at home with her two children, Owen and Daisy
and her furbaby Barney.
Shes is currently in a relationship with David.

Lightning Source UK Ltd.
Milton Keynes UK
UKHW020638290121
377903UK00011B/790